MEDITATION JOURNAL

CHIMI CHANTÉ

COPYRIGHT

© 2021 SHI-CHI, Unincorporated
Published by SHI-CHI, Unincorporated
Los Angeles, California 90292

All rights reserved. No portion of this book may be reproduced, stored in retrieval system, or transmitted in any form or by any means-electronic, mechanical, photocopy, recording, scanning, or other--except for brief quotations in critical review or articles, without the prior written permission of the publisher.

Meditation Journal is a registered trademark of SHI-CHI, Unincorporated, All rights reserved.

This publication is designed to provided accurate and authorized information with regard to the subject matter covered. It is sold with the understanding that the publication is not engaged in rendering professional advise. If professional advise or other experts assistance is required, the services of a competent professional should be sought.

Editors: NSU Prints

Cover Design: NSU Prints

Interior Design: NSU Prints
ISBN: 9798785227934

DEDICATION

I dedicate this book to you!
I personally thank you for allowing me to assist you
in your journey to becoming more mindful
and choosing to gift yourself your very own attention.
You deserve it. Happy journaling!

A SIMPLE GUIDE TO
MEITATION

*"True beauty emanates from an unseen place.
Close your eyes and go within
to uncover the beauty in all things"*
~ Chimi Chanté

I believe that one of the highest forms of self-love is honoring yourself with a full presence, and that meditation is the kindest act that you could possibly give to yourself. It is the gift that keeps on giving. Not only do you benefit from this kind gesture but those around you who share space and heartbeats will also.

Meditation is engaging in mental exercise for the purpose of reaching heighten awareness. It is a way to become conscious of the thoughts, feelings, and emotions that are creating your future. There is no wrong or right way to meditate. Your meditation is specific to you. However, awareness is the starting point. All forms of meditation is simply about a sense of self-awareness. It is about being conscious of your thoughts and your perception of the world around you. There is power in gaining control over your thoughts and this power allows you to pattern your life after your them.

To gain control of your life you must gain power over your mind. You can mind your thoughts with the active use of a routine meditation practice. When meditation is practiced regularly one of its promising benefits is the ability to exercise Mind-Over-Matter. You develop the ability to consciously choose your thoughts, rather than allowing your thoughts to control you. Meditation has also proven to be most effective in promoting health mentally and physically, transcending negative emotions, and activating a balanced life. With the use of these simple and practical instructions you can learn to use meditation as a tool to ultimate control and to create rapid progress that will benefit you in all areas of your life.

1. Affirm Your Intention. Intention simply put is a vision. Vision inspires you to give your very best and shapes your understanding of why you are doing what you do. For example before beginning your meditation practice get into the conscious habit of asking yourself, "What do I want to accomplish?" If is to change your mood from experiencing thoughts of anxiety, set your intention to replace your thoughts of anxiety with thoughts of serenity and peace.

2. Pick A Time. Meditation improves quality of life in the long run. You only need a few minutes of your day. Pick a time and a gentle alarm to use as a timer.

3. Sit In A Quiet Area & Comfortable Position. You don't need a special environment or equipment in order to practice meditation. However, this helps prevent distractions and interruptions during your meditation.

4. Close Your Eyes. Closing your eyes during meditation helps you to block out the outside. This creates a sharper focus and better concentration.

5. Be Still. Sitting for moments in a routine meditation practice in stillness and quietude not only allows you to take better control of your life but also trains your focus to witness beauty and order within the seeming chaos.

6. Bring Your Attention To Your Breath. Focusing on your breathing helps to center you and places you in the present moment creating more of a mindful experience.

7. Don't Be Discouraged. Don't be hard on yourself if you notice your mind beginning to wander. Allow your thoughts to serve you by simply observing them without judgement. Then bring your attention back to your breath.

8. Surrender. Meditation is a spiritual surrender that places you into complete receptivity with source. This sweet surrender is what I refer to as "Touching Your Soul". Surrendering to the mystery of "here and now" provides you with mental clarity and deepens your connection to experience a more soulful and fulfilling union with source. This opens you up to receive supreme inner wisdom and guidance.

9. Journal About Your Experience. Journaling as a whole is a healthy route to healing emotionally, psychologically, and physically. It allows you to connect more intimately with yourself while also documenting your healing. Journaling creates an opportunity for you to record your insight after your meditation practice. It is good to capture this immediately after your meditation so that you are be able to retain it and begin the use of applying the insight in your life. Application is the true transforming operative power.

10. Be Gentle With Yourself. Keep in mind that meditation like mastering any new skill takes time and you are worthy of both your time and patience. Simply start by creating a daily routine to practice meditation for at least a few moments a day. Your patience and persistence throughout your practice will help increase your progress and meditation will prove to be a miraculous journey to your best you yet!
I have created a series of guided meditations that you may follow along with on my mindfulness blog www.MindBodyBeyond.org. You may also access the guided

ABOUT THE AUTHOR

Chimi Chanté is commonly known for *"...and so it is written."*, her inspirational journal collection that spreads warm and positive messages throughout the entire collection. She is also the founder of an uplifting mindfulness blog MindBodyBeyond.org. Her focus is in a full transformative process through the use of a routine spiritual practices by use of ;meditation, affirmations, and introspection. She has mentored closely under the guidance of Sufi Master Teacher Dr. Chiboola Malaambo, as well as studied under the teachings of New Thought Minister Reverend Dr. Michael Bernard Beckwith; Founder of the Agape International Spiritual Center. Chimi is also the proud mother of three beautiful, talented, and gifted children whom she credits for being the motivating force behind all of her success and accomplishments. Please visit www.ChimiChanté.com for more information on her transformative products and services.

Made in the USA
Columbia, SC
06 October 2024

7cdda3da-975a-4fb9-a636-749d883c2f01R01